My Weekend With Papi

Text by Tony Plata
Illustrations by Treal Toonz

ISBN 978-1666401646 (Paperback)
ISBN 979-8369265246 (Hardcover)
LCCN-2023910463

First edition 2023

Preface

As a non-custodial parent, I share many beautiful memories with my children. I want the reader to understand that the bond between parent and child is unbreakable and the most important thing is time spent together. All children are loved, even if they do not always live with both parents.

Dedication

To my children, Diego, Taina, Mariano, and Gabriel, I am blessed
to be your father.
Thank you for creating so many beautiful moments with me.
To all the children who don't live with both parents, know that you
are loved!

Acknowledgments

I would like to thank Alexander Prezioso and Luz Maria Mack for their guidance in creating this book. To the team at Chosen Veterans Publishing, especially Clavia Allen for her dedication to helping me see my vision become reality.

Hola friends! My name is Mateo. My mom and dad say that I am growing up in a "unique" situation and that they love me so much.

I live with my mom, but I get to see my dad during the week.
I also get to stay over with my dad in my other house over the weekends.

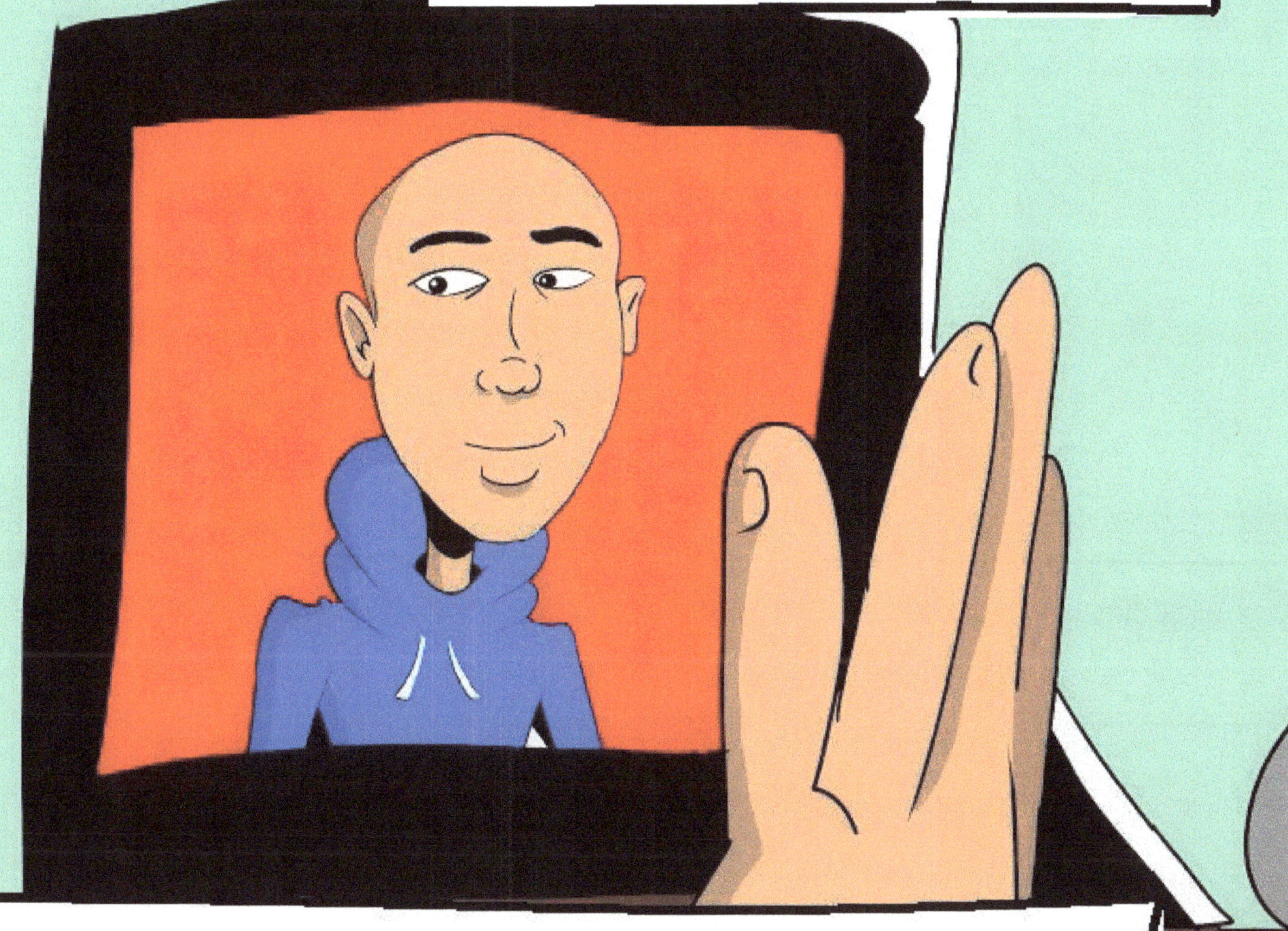

This is my dad, and I call him papi.
I keep this picture of him in my room. Even when we are not together, I can wish my papi a good night.

At my mom's house, I have my "time with papi" calendar on the refrigerator.
I can count the days until I can stay over with papi again.

Each day I mark the calendar to keep track of when I get to stay over with him again.
M T W T F S
Today is very exciting because it is Friday. I will get to spend the weekend with my papi.

Today after school papi is going to pick me up.
I wonder what fun things we will do together this weekend.

Maybe papi and I will do something really fun.
I hope we go to the park to play baseball.

ELEMENTARY
Every Friday papi comes to school to pick me up. I bet he is counting the minutes waiting for me to be dismissed.

I love when he picks me up from school.
I get so excited that I will run and dodge around my friends to quickly meet with my papi.

Every time I get into papi's car, he always reminds me to buckle up.
He will not start the car until I have my seatbelt on.

He loves and misses me so much that he moves the rear-view mirror to see my smiling face.
I really enjoy spending the weekend with my papi.

When we drive to his house, we always get stuck in traffic.
I wonder if there are any other kids traveling to see their other parents.

I always have the GPS running on my toy phone to help papi keep track of the traffic.
Papi, let's use the super-fast button to get home! "VVVrrrrmmmmmmmm!"

Sometimes on our way to papi's house, we play the counting game. Papi says, "let's count all of the blue trucks we see."
We count the numbers in our heads then compare them. Our numbers are never the same and we always laugh about it.

3
4
5
2
6
7
1
8
9

In the car, I get to hear my
favorite songs on the radio.

When the music plays, I snap my fingers to the beat and sing.

When we get to papi's house, we get things ready for dinner.
We always make delicious food.

When papi makes dinner, we always cook together. I hand him all the ingredients to cook.
What is your favorite food for dinner?

After we eat dinner, I always help clean up in the kitchen.

Papi and I are such a great team when cleaning up.

After dinner, we get to play my favorite game, dominoes. Papi is such a good player.

JUICE

Papi and I always match the numbers.
We play several games, and I keep trying to win against him.

After playing dominoes, it is time for bed.
I get changed into my pajamas and brush my teeth.

Tomorrow is Saturday, and I have a baseball game.
I am so excited that papi will be there to watch me play.

During the game, I always try to do my best.
I know I can hit the ball if I focus.

Papi always cheers me on when it is my turn to bat.
I can hear him shout, "come on Mateo, you can do it, hit the ball!"

On Sundays, papi and I love
to play board games.

At papi's house, I have so many toys to play with.
I have a lot of fun adventures with my dinosaurs and robots.

ELEMENTARY
On Monday morning, papi drops me off at school.

How was your weekend?
At school, I get to tell all of my friends about the wonderful time I had over the weekend with my papi.

THE END

A note from the Author

According to an article written by the Annie E. Casey Foundation, *Child Well-Being in Single-Parent Families, in the United States,* nearly 24 million children live in a single parent home. While close to 15 million, live in mother-only households, approximately 3 to 4 million live in father-only households. 64% of African American children and 40% of Latino children are most likely to live in a single-parent household. After a divorce or parental breakup, children often spend less time with their nonresident parent. Maintaining an involved, nurturing relationship with the noncustodial parent is very important for a child's well-being.

As a non-custodial parent, I want to share the experiences I have with my children when they are with me. The time apart from my children weighs heavily on me, as well as for them. I want to normalize this type of bond children have with their non-custodial parent as they are loved no matter what.

ABOUT THE AUTHOR

Tony Plata is a Bronx born author and a United States Army Veteran. He is the father of four children. His stories are about his relationships with his children and the importance of being a supportive co-parent. He shares with his readers, the many beautiful experiences, and adventures they share when they are together. Tony has earned a Master of Science in Education from Lehman College (TESOL) and a Master of Science in Education from the City College of New York (School Administration). He is currently serving on military active duty in the New York City Tri-State area.

- Tony Plata

About the Book

My Weekend with Papi is about the emotional joy both parent and child feel in anticipation of spending time together. The story shows how a boy, and his father are excited to spend time with each other. The son marks the days off on his calendar in anticipation of spending the weekend with his father. The father feels anxious waiting to pick up his son from school. They both love spending the weekend together bonding over things like cooking, cleaning, and playing games. As a very supportive parent, the father is his child's number one fan during baseball games. The story ends with the son asking his classmates how they spent their weekend.

This book is intended for children from ages 2-8 years (PK-3rd grade).

Resources Page for Fathers

https://www.uaufatherhoodmatters.org
https://www.nyc.gov/site/dycd/services/family-support/fatherhood-initiative.page
https://www.fatherhood.gov